D0605819

FIESTA!

ENGLAND

GROLIER
EDUCATIONAL

Published 1999 by Grolier Educational
Sherman Turnpike, Danbury, Connecticut.
Copyright © 1999 Times Editions Pte Ltd. Singapore.

Set ISBN: 0-7172-9324-6
Volume ISBN: 0-7172-9329-7

CIP information available from the Library of Congress or the publisher

Brown Partworks Ltd.

Series Editor: Tessa Paul
Series Designer: Joyce Mason
Crafts devised and created by Susan Moxley
Music arrangements by Harry Boteler
Photographs by Bruce Mackie
Production: Alex Mackenzie
Stylists: Joyce Mason and Tessa Paul

For this volume:
Editorial Assistants: Hannah Beardon and Paul Thompson

Printed in Italy

Adult supervision advised for all crafts and recipes, particularly those involving sharp instruments and heat.

CONTENTS

ENGLAND:

England is part of an island off the coast of Europe. The island is surrounded by the English Channel to the south and the North Sea to the east. The North Atlantic Ocean lies to the north and the Irish Sea to the west.

▶**This yellow stone village,** with thatched roofs on some of its houses, is typical of an area of England called the Cotswolds. The English countryside is noted for its picturesque villages.

North Atlantic Ocean

Northern Ireland

First Impressions

- **Population** 51,439,200
- **Largest city** London with a population of 9,227,687
- **Longest river** River Severn
- **Highest mountain** Scafell Pike at 3,227 ft.
- **Exports** Machinery, manufactured goods, vehicles, and textiles
- **Capital city** London
- **Political status** Constitutional monarchy
- **Climate** Wet and cool for most of the year
- **Art and culture** England is renowned for its writers. One of the greatest writers in the world was English — William Shakespeare.

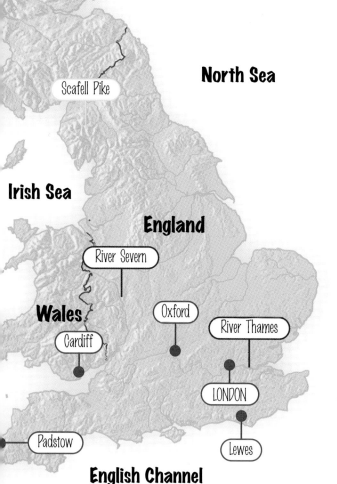

Scotland

North Sea

Scafell Pike

Irish Sea

England

River Severn

Wales

Oxford

River Thames

Cardiff

LONDON

Padstow

Lewes

English Channel

◀**The Norman Conquest** of 1066 was the last time England was invaded. The Normans came from northern France and brought with them their distinctive style of architecture, with its square towers and rounded windows. Many old churches in England still have their Norman towers.

▲**Big Ben** was built in 1859. It is one of the important landmarks of England's capital city, London. The clock is famous for its accuracy and for its distinctive chime. The sound has often been copied by clock makers. Big Ben was designed by Edmund Beckett and named after Sir Benjamin Hall, who was responsible for government buildings when the clock was made.

RELIGIONS

In England the head of the national church is also the head of state. This is unusual in Europe and the Americas. This form of government grew from a religious quarrel in the sixteenth century.

ENGLAND is a Christian country. This means the beliefs of the people are based on the teachings of Christ. He was born 2,000 years ago in the Middle East. His ideas spread across Europe, and Christianity was accepted in England about 700 years after His birth.

Early Christians were led by priests. They, in turn, were guided by bishops. The head bishop was called the pope, whose base was in Rome. However, in 1534 an important English king, Henry VIII, wanted to divorce his wife. The church did not allow divorce. Henry refused to obey the pope, so he declared England free of the pope's authority. He made himself head of the Church of England. Henry divorced his wife, and there is still a law ruling that no English monarch can be a Roman Catholic.

At the time Henry broke away from Rome, there were many religious reformers. They, too, rejected the authority of the pope. They also wanted to change certain Christian beliefs and rituals. Because they were making a protest they were called "Protestants."

Over the next 200 years there was great strife between those people who remained loyal to the pope, those who wanted the monarch to control the church, and those Protestants who wanted neither pope nor monarch. This strife affected Scotland and Ireland. In Ireland the effects of the strife are felt to the present day.

The English people learned to be wary of strong religious feelings. They accepted that people could choose their own religion and that it was not a crime to reject the Church of England.

Some of the English attend other Protestant churches, such as the Presbytarian, Baptist, and Methodist churches. Some have stayed loyal to the Roman Catholic Church.

After the religious wars stopped, the English turned their energies to trade. They grew so powerful that, by 1900, they ruled over many areas of the world.

People in Asia, Africa, and the Americas were all part of this great empire.

After World War II the empire broke up, often in chaos and unrest. People from Asia and Africa went to England. Many were not Christian, and they brought other faiths, such as Islam and Hinduism, into the country. Jews have lived for centuries in England.

GREETINGS FROM **ENGLAND!**

The English live in the United Kingdom. The Scots, the Welsh, and the people of Northern Ireland also live in the United Kingdom. All these people are known as British, and they all speak English. In Scotland and Ireland a few people speak Gaelic, an old language that used to be spoken by everyone in these two places. The people of Wales try to keep their old tongue, Welsh, alive, and schools in Wales hold classes in Welsh and English.

For 300 years, starting in the seventeenth century, the British built up the biggest empire known in history. In doing so they spread the English language across the world. Their first colonies were in North America. By 1900 the empire included Hong Kong, Singapore, India, parts of South America, Canada, Australia, the Caribbean islands, and large parts of Africa.

MAY DAY

On May 1 people celebrate the end of winter and the coming of spring. They parade, dance, and sing in the streets. In some towns special performers called Morris Dancers put on a show.

Celebrations on May Day are very old. In England there is a stained glass church window that shows a maypole with people dancing around it. The window is 1,000 years old. Even now this day is celebrated with maypoles, music, dancing, and merriment.

May Day is a time of joy. It marks the end of winter and brings with it the hopes of a good, rich harvest. For many thousands of years people did not really understand how plants grew or how the land worked so

When children dance around the maypole, they hold colored ribbons. The ribbons weave together in a pretty pattern.

"Pearly Kings and Queens" cover their suits in buttons cut from oyster shells ("mother of pearl"). In London they take part in street events such as May Day.

8

they felt that rituals, dances, and games on May Day helped the land to produce crops.

The maypole was a symbol of growth. In London and the other great cities of England there used to be permanent maypoles erected in the streets.

Nowadays these poles are put up for the day only. The maypole is tall – some are 80 feet high. Colored ribbons are attached to the top, and children dance around the pole, each holding a ribbon.

There are villages where one of the girls may be chosen to be "May Queen." She is the sign of spring.

Some towns have other special customs. In Hastings, a town in southern England, a man covers his head and body in a hard suit of wicker-woven twigs. This suit is then covered with greenery and flowers until you can only see his eyes. He is called "Jack in the Green," and he represents summer.

HERE WE GO GATHERING NUTS IN MAY

This is a song traditionally sung by children while they dance, weaving their colorful ribbons around a village maypole.

Whom will you have for nuts in May,

nuts in May, nuts in May?

Whom will you have for nuts in May,

all on a fro - sty mor - ning?

After the verse (left) the children sing the chorus to the same tune:
"Here we go gathering nuts in May, nuts in May, nuts in May.
Here we go gathering nuts in May. All on a frosty morning."

Morris Dancers wear colorful ribbons on their costumes. As drums and pipes play, the men dance over sticks placed on the ground.

People follow him as he parades through the streets of the town. In Padstow, in southwestern England, a man dresses as a horse on May Day. He hides under a frame covered with black cloth. He is called the "'obby 'oss" (hobby horse). He runs and jumps around the town. From time to time the "'oss" tries to capture a woman from the crowd. If he manages to catch her, people say she will have a baby in the next year. The hobby horse has been part of the May Day fun for hundreds of years. No one is sure why it became part of May Day. Perhaps it was because those early people believed he brought the summer.

Groups of men called Morris Dancers are part of May Day, and their leaping dance routines often tell stories. A favorite dance is about Robin

The Morris Dancers tie bells on their legs. The steps of the dance are designed to make the bells ring as the dancers stamp and jump.

church bells ring, and people drink glasses of champagne. Then they follow the Morris Dancers as they leap through the streets of the town.

Hood, Maid Marian, and their band of men – folk heroes who robbed the rich to help the poor.

In Oxford, central England, there is a famous old university. Early on May Day morning a choir from Magdalen College, a part of the university, climbs up a tall church tower near the river. Sitting in boats or crowded on a nearby bridge, people wait for six o'clock when the Magdalen choir sings a hymn. As the singers finish, the

EGG SANDWICHES

INGREDIENTS
12 slices brown bread
3 eggs, hard-boiled
2 T. mayonnaise
1 package watercress, snipped
½ t. salt
¼ t. pepper

Peel the eggs, being sure to remove all the shell. In a small bowl mash the eggs with the back of a fork. Add the mayonnaise and salt. Lay six pieces of bread on the counter. Put an equal amount of egg salad onto each slice. Spread evenly, then sprinkle with watercress. Place the top slices on the sandwiches and press down gently. Trim off edges. Cut into triangles.

ROBIN OF SHERWOOD

*Many stories are told about brave Robin Hood
and his merry band of men. This one is about
Robin and Maid Marian – a story acted by
the Morris Dancers.*

THE WICKED OSWALD Montdragon forced Maid Marian to travel with him into Sherwood Forest. He wanted Marian to charm and trick the outlaw Robin Hood. Montdragon wanted the big reward offered for the capture of Robin.

Marian had heard Robin was no outlaw. He robbed the rich, not for his own gain, but to feed the poor. He was a great lord by birth, but he preferred to live free in the forest. The maid did not want to be part of some awful trick to catch him. She was glad when her carriage was halted by a handsome stranger who chased Oswald Montdragon away. She sobbed and told the stranger how Montdragon would put her, and her own dear mother, in prison if she did not help arrest Robin. She begged the man to hide her.

The stranger insisted she go home to her mother. His men rode her to the castle where Montdragon and her mother lived. There, Marian found sadness and horror. Her mother was dead, and the wicked Montdragon tried to force Marian to marry him.

One night Marian dressed as a boy. She picked a strong horse and rode deep into the forest. However, when a tall man sprang out of the trees, she was terrified. She waved her sword at him, but he told her she was too small a boy to fight. Marian knew this was the voice of the stranger. "I am not a boy," she cried. "I am Maid Marian."

"And I am Robin Hood," answered the stranger.

Maid Marian and Robin Hood married and lived happily together in the forest.

TROOPING THE COLOR

This event marks the birthday of the monarch. It is not the actual birth date. Real birthdays often fell in months of bad weather, so officials decreed June a suitable month to celebrate a monarch's birthday.

This royal pageant first occurred 250 years ago, in 1755, to celebrate the birthday of a prince. Since 1959 it has happened on a Saturday in June chosen to mark the official birthday of the monarch.

In olden days the soldiers went to war on foot or on horseback. They often fought hand-to-hand with the enemy. Each regiment, or group of soldiers, carried its own color. In the chaos of battle the sight of this flag made sure men did not get lost. In the British army there is a section called the Household Division. It has eight regiments. Six of them are on foot. The remaining two regiments are cavalry. They are on horses.

Each year one of the regiments shows its color to the monarch. Bands play, cannons fire a salute, and all eight regiments of the Household Division troop in front of the queen. Crowds gather to watch the show in London.

THE ROYAL CALENDAR

Many celebrations in England are not fixed on the calendar. The dates are decided by events in the life of the royal family. Weddings, funerals, and anniversaries bring the people of England together. In 1977 the English held street parties, and the government arranged impressive state events, because Queen Elizabeth had been queen for 25 years. The day was treated as her 25th "birthday" as queen. It was called her "Silver Jubilee." On these occasions the queen travels in a special state coach. Her husband, Prince Philip, is usually at her side. She is very fond of corgi dogs, and in this model of her coach one of these little dogs can be seen trotting behind.

GREENSLEEVES

This English folk song may have been written by King Henry VIII. He ruled England from 1509 to 1547 and had six wives. Henry loved music and was said to sing well. The man in the song is sad because his girlfriend no longer loves him.

MAKE A COMMEMORATIVE PLATE AND MUG

Commemorative china is designed to mark a special occasion. You, too, can make a lasting reminder of an important event.

The tradition of decorating china to mark important events began in England in the 1830s. Potters painted jugs and mugs that celebrated the coronation of Queen Victoria. These proved so popular that similar products were made for the queen's birthday. Potteries did not stop at royal occasions. Sporting occasions, wars, and political events were commemorated on china. The English continue to make commemorative ware for all occasions, but most especially for royal celebrations. This kind of chinaware is eagerly collected by many people.

YOU WILL NEED
A pencil
A plate or mug
Tracing paper
Carbon paper
Ceramic paints
Tape

1 Cut tracing paper to fit your plate. With a pencil draw your design onto paper. Fit a sheet of carbon paper to the back of the tracing paper so that your design is on top.

2 Hold tracing paper and carbon paper together. Position them on the plate so carbon side is on the plate, tracing paper on top. Fix to the plate with adhesive tape. Use a pencil to trace the design. Remove tracing and carbon paper. Your design marks the china.

3 Using one color, paint in the outlines. Let it dry. Paint in the design. Let each color dry before using the next. Add a border if you wish.

DESIGNS FOR YOUR CHINA

Commemorative china can carry a portrait of the person involved in an important event. In England the face of the queen is used often. Sometimes heraldic designs are shown. *Heraldic* means the signs used to identify noble people, clubs, or armies. Lions and unicorns are found in heraldic designs. You may want to commemorate something important in your life. You can paint words, names, or dates on your china. Check if your ceramic paint needs to be baked or fired.

SAINT DAVID'S DAY

People in Wales, to the west of England, celebrate the traditions of their country on March 1. They remember a great Welsh Christian, Saint David, who died on this day almost 1,500 years ago.

Wales is famous for its music and – most especially – its choirs. All over Wales on Saint David's Day you will find choirs performing. Some of them have flown in from far across the world to be in Wales on Saint David's Day.

A special type of choir popular in Wales is the "male voice choir." One of the main events on Saint David's Day is a huge concert in the Welsh capital city, Cardiff, by a male voice choir with 1,000 singers. In many towns people compete

People may pin a daffodil to their coat to mark Saint David's Day. In olden days the flower was linked to renewal of life. Also, it is thought to have calming powers.

in festivals of singing, dancing, and reciting poems. They are called *Eisteddfodau* in Welsh.

Many people in the country cannot speak Welsh. However, Welsh is taught in the schools.

Saint David's Day is specially remembered in the schools of Wales. On this day children put on the traditional clothes of Wales. Girls wear tall hats, and the boys wear white shirts with frills at the neck and the wrists. Their

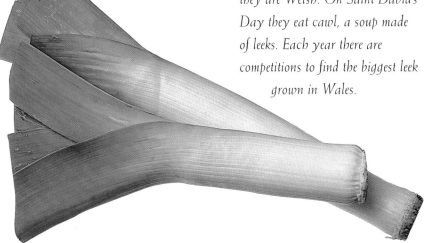

People wear a leek as a sign that they are Welsh. On Saint David's Day they eat cawl, a soup made of leeks. Each year there are competitions to find the biggest leek grown in Wales.

black trousers stop at the knee, and they wear long wool socks. They march from school to the local church for a service to remember their saint. Afterward they take part in a school version of the *Eisteddfodau.*

People go on pilgrimages to the saint's shrine in the town named after him. The Welsh also pin leeks to their clothes on Saint David's Day.

Many stories try to explain why the leek is connected to this saint. After all, when he was made a saint, David's sign was a dove. One story claims David told Welshmen to wear a leek in their hats during a battle against their Saxon enemy. They did as they were told and won the day. In the Welsh regiments of the British army the soldiers eat a raw leek on Saint David's Day.

This doll wears a traditional Welsh girl's costume. The petticoat she wears under her dress is made of a special Welsh flannel, a soft cloth woven from wool. The tall hat is called a "beaver hat." Girls dress in this costume to take part in Saint David's Day parades.

SAINT DAVID

Saint David is called Dewi Sant in Welsh. He was born in southwest Wales around A.D. 520. His father was a Welsh prince. As a boy David went to live in a monastery, where Christian monks, a special group of priests, live and study. Later David became a missionary — someone who teaches his own faith to others. David founded, or set up, several churches in Wales. He also founded a monastery at Rose Vale in southwest Wales, where the town of Saint David's is today. David ate only vegetables and drank nothing but water. He was a very great missionary who spread the word of Christ around Wales. In 1120 the Roman Catholic pope Gallactacus made David a saint — a holy person.

HARVEST FESTIVAL

In the fall people bring offerings of food to church to thank God for the harvest – the gathering of crops in the country fields. They sing hymns and sometimes hold a celebration meal.

The church is beautifully decorated for harvest festival. At the front, where everyone can see them, baskets of vegetables and bowls of flowers surround the altar, the table used for ritual offerings. In some churches fruits such as apples and plums are laid out in lines on the window sills. In the country sheaves of barley or wheat lean against the walls.

Christian Harvest replaced ancient festivals, too old to be given a date. For thousands of years most people lived off the land, growing their own food. At the end of summer, when the crops were cut and lifted from the earth, those early English harvesters sang and danced, and shouted their joy. They used to cover their houses in branches. The last sheaf of corn was woven into a "dolly" and sprinkled with water as a rain charm.

The Harvest Festival service is held on a Sunday. On the day before the service people decorate the church with flowers and baskets of fruits and vegetables.

20

These old customs slowly moved into the church and, even now, corn dollies may be seen among the festive fruits and vegetables.

Old harvest songs became hymns with a harvest theme. Special services , were developed to mark the end of the harvest. During these services the priest asks God to bless all the food. Then everyone enjoys a "Harvest Home" meal held, not in the church itself, but in a hall that belongs to the church.

Churchgoers bring their home-cooked food to share.

Nowadays very few people grow their own food. Modern festivals show vegetables and fruits grown by a few folk, but most church-goers offer bought foodstuffs. After the service the food that decorated the church is given to those who do not have enough to feed themselves.

Many fruits – including apples – are harvested in fall in England. People often bring homemade fruit jams or vegetable pickles and chutneys to offer at church. They may pick colorful plants to brighten up the church hall if they are having a "Harvest Home" – a celebratory meal.

MAKE A CORN DOLLY

Experts can twist wheat into shapes of women, donkeys, and birds. Whatever shape they are, all are called "corn dollies." Make your own fun corn dolly.

In 1598 a traveler in England described a girl-doll made of corn. He saw it at a Harvest Festival. On stone tablets in some very old churches there are carvings of braided corn. These are much the same design as this straw dolly that you can make yourself.

YOU WILL NEED
4 stalks of wheat
24" of thread
¼" width colored ribbon

1 Take four stalks of wheat and cut each at the first notch from the head. Remove the loose leaves and, with the thread, tie the heads of the four stalks together. Do not cut the loose end of thread.

2 Holding your palm upward, push the wheat between the index and middle fingers so that the heads are hanging down, the stalks sticking up. The tie is between your fingers. Close to the tie fold the stalks of wheat so that one points North (N), one points West (W), one points South (S), and one East (E).

N

W

E

S

4 Bend the braided stalks into a loop. Using the loose ends of the thread, tie the end of the braiding just below the head. Tie a ribbon around the thread to hide it and to decorate your "corn dolly." Hang one dolly on a door or arrange two or three in a pretty bunch.

3 Now bend the north-facing stalk to the south; the south to the north; the west to the east, and the east to the west. Continue doing this braiding until you have about an inch of unbraided straw left.

Back view

BONFIRE NIGHT

When night falls on November 5, the sky lights up with fireworks. In gardens and parks people crowd around the bonfires and eat hot snacks to keep warm.

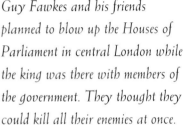

Bonfire Night recalls an event almost 400 years old. In 1605 a gang led by Robert Catesby and Guy Fawkes laid plans to kill James I, the king of England, with gunpowder. This explosion was planned for November 5. Guy was a Roman Catholic who wished to murder the non-Catholic king, but he was arrested before he could do so.

Guy Fawkes and his friends planned to blow up the Houses of Parliament in central London while the king was there with members of the government. They thought they could kill all their enemies at once.

BAKED POTATOES

INGREDIENTS
*6 medium potatoes,
washed and dried
Tin foil
6 T. of butter
6 sprigs of parsley*

Cut the foil into squares about 6" x 6". Pierce each potato with a fork, then wrap it in foil. Place in the oven and bake for 45 minutes, or until soft in the center when pierced with a fork. To serve, open out foil, being careful not to burn yourself. Cut a cross in the top of each potato, squeeze to open, and top with a pat of butter and a sprig of parsley.

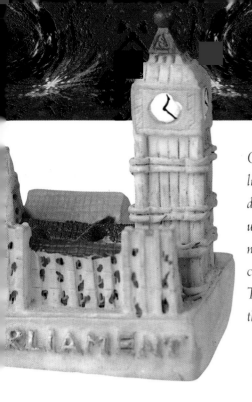

Guys are no longer made to look like Guy Fawkes. They are dressed in any old clothes. People used to stuff them with straw, but nowadays townspeople use crumpled pieces of newspaper. These guys burn up quickly in the bonfire flames.

During the festivities on Bonfire Night people throw straw men – named "guys" after Guy Fawkes – onto bonfires. They let off fireworks to recall the explosives that the Catholic plotters had with them. One town, Lewes, flings not only a "guy" onto the fire but a straw pope too. The people do this in memory of 17 local Protestants who were burned to death by Roman Catholics in the terrible religious wars of 400 years ago.

Many people build bonfires in their own gardens, make guys from old clothes, and light their own fireworks. The occasion is a party, and people eat potatoes baked in embers – the glowing remains of the fire.

In most towns and cities there are public Bonfire Nights in the parks, where wood is stacked to make huge bonfires, and grand displays of fireworks are given.

25

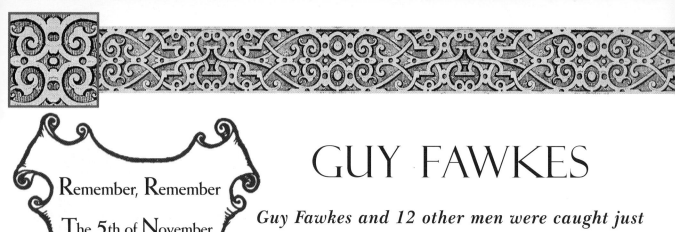

GUY FAWKES

Guy Fawkes and 12 other men were caught just a few hours before they were going to blow up the Houses of Parliament and kill James I. They had kept their plan secret for weeks.

Remember, Remember
The 5th of November,
Gunpowder,
Treason and Plot!

GUY FAWKES AND his friends were determined to kill King James I because the king claimed he was head of the Church of England. Guy was a Roman Catholic. He believed that the pope in Rome was head of the church. There were other Englishmen who felt the same way as Guy. They wanted to replace James with a Catholic monarch.

A man called Robert Catesby had the idea of blowing up the king with gunpowder. He persuaded four other men, including Guy, to join him in his secret plot.

Catesby knew that each fall the king and his government ministers met in the Houses of Parliament in London for a big ceremony. He told the plotters: "If we explode the gunpowder under Parliament, we will kill all our enemies at once." They found an empty cellar in the depths of Parliament. It was the perfect place to set the gunpowder.
Guy and his

cronies did not say why they wanted the cellar. The keeper of the cellar told them they must pay to use the room.

The gang did not have enough money to pay this rent. They asked other Catholics to help them. One of these people was a man called Francis Tresham. Now, Francis had relatives who happened also to be members of Parliament. The bomb might kill them. Francis begged the plotters to scrap their dreadful plan, but they refused. Then someone sent a letter about the plot to Francis's family, and they ran to

the king. Guy was caught on November 4, the very day before the planned attack. He suffered a horrible death. The law courts ordered that Guy be hung, drawn, and quartered.

The frightened people showed loyalty to their king. Bonfires were lit and a straw figure of Guy was thrown onto one fire. Every year the English repeat the events that followed Guy's arrest.

CHRISTMAS

Christmas Day, December 25, comes in the middle of winter in England. Children hope for a "white Christmas" – with a layer of snow making the trees look pretty – but they are often disappointed.

Christmas marks the day when Jesus Christ was born 2,000 years ago. During the evening, in the weeks just before Christmas, people go from door to door, and they sing carols, the songs that celebrate the birth of Jesus Christ.

In schools across the country children perform in a "nativity play." These plays tell the story of the birth of Jesus, who was born in a humble stable.

Weeks before Christmas people make a special fruit cake for the day. They cover it with marzipan – a paste of almond, nuts, and eggs – and a layer of white icing. Decorations add a final touch.

In London the central city streets are richly decorated with neon lights. Crowds gather to watch a member of the royal family, or perhaps some other public figure, switch on the lights for this very festive season.

Christians attend church at Christmas. Families with children prefer to visit their church on Christmas morning, but many English people go to services held at midnight on Christmas Eve.

In England most families choose to be

together at Christmas to share a festive meal. As in other Christian countries, people in England buy a fir tree to put in their homes. They decorate it with lights and tinsel. At the foot of the tree families pile all their presents.

Children dangle stockings from their beds on Christmas Eve. They believe that Father Christmas flies through the sky on a sleigh pulled by reindeer. He stops at every house to fill each child's stocking with Christmas gifts.

The children often leave

Mistletoe (above) symbolizes goodness. During the festivities people stand beneath it to kiss. Holly (below) was used as decoration by early Christians.

a carrot, or straw, as a gift for the reindeer. On Christmas Day the family sits around the tree to open all their presents together.

The festive meal is usually at midday, and it is the tradition to eat roast turkey. At the table the guests wear funny paper hats and they pull crackers, tubes of paper that make a small bang when pulled.

Christmas pudding ends the meal. A few small coins are mixed into the pudding. It is supposed to be lucky to find one of these in your helping.

Christmas pudding is wrapped in cloth and foil, then boiled. Before it is served, brandy is poured over it and set alight. The flames flicker briefly, then the pudding is eaten.

GLORIOUS FOURTH

This festival was started in 1793 to celebrate the birthday of the English king George III. It takes place at Eton College, a famous school in the town of Windsor.

Eton College, where they hold the Glorious Fourth of June festival, was founded more than 500 years ago. Only boys attend the school. The main part of the festival is the "Procession of Boats." Ten boats parade on the river. The boys in the boats wear straw hats decorated with flowers. At the end of the parade these hats are raised to Eton, to the nearby castle of Windsor, and to the queen. A major cricket match is played while family and friends picnic in the grounds.

WORDS TO KNOW

Altar: A table on which worshippers leave offerings, burn incense, or perform ceremonies.

Colony: A land that is ruled by people from another country.

Carol: A joyful song, usually performed at Christmas.

Cavalry: Soldiers on horseback.

Eisteddfodau: Welsh festivals in which contests of singing, dancing, and poetry-reciting take place.

Hymn: A song of praise to God.

Mass: A Christian ritual in which bread and wine are used to commemorate the Last Supper of Jesus Christ.

Missionary: A person who travels to a foreign land with the aim of converting others to his or her religion.

Monastery: A place where monks live in a religious community.

Monk: A man who devotes his life to his religion and lives in a monastery.

Parliament: A group of men and women chosen by the people of the United Kingdom to make laws and decide on other important matters.

Pilgrim: A person who makes a religious journey, or pilgrimage, to a holy place.

Protestant: A member of one of the Protestant churches, which all together form one of the main branches of Christianity. The Protestants split from the Roman Catholic Church in the sixteenth century.

Regiment: A group of soldiers who live and fight together.

Roman Catholic: A member of the Roman Catholic Church, the largest branch of Christianity. The head of this church is the pope.

Saint: A title given to very holy people by some Christian churches. Saints are important in the Roman Catholic Church.

Saxons: An ancient European people, one of the main ancestors of the English.

ACKNOWLEDGMENTS

WITH THANKS TO:

Guards Museum, London.
Pollock's Toy Museum, London.
Morris Dancing Equipment, London.
Guy Fawkes model by Zoë Paul.

PHOTOGRAPHY:

All photographs by Bruce Mackie except: Marshall Cavendish pp. 11, 24. Cover photograph by Katie Vandyk.

ILLUSTRATIONS BY:

Fiona Saunders pp. 4 – 5. Tracy Rich p. 7. Maps by John Woolford.

Recipes: Ellen Dupont.

SET CONTENTS